by Iain Gray

Lang**Syne**

PUBLISHING

WRITING *to* REMEMBER

79 Main Street, Newtongrange,
Midlothian EH22 4NA
Tel: 0131 344 0414   Fax: 0845 075 6085
E-mail: info@lang-syne.co.uk
www.langsyneshop.co.uk

Design by Dorothy Meikle
Printed by Ricoh Print Scotland
© Lang Syne Publishers Ltd 2014

ISBN 978-1-85217-518-4

Hunt

MOTTO:
I accomplish my course.

CREST:
A hound with an antique crown
(and)
The head of a lion
(and)
The head of a hind.

NAME variations include:
Huntar
Hunter

Chapter one:

The origins of popular surnames

by George Forbes and Iain Gray

If you don't know where you came from, you won't know where you're going is a frequently quoted observation and one that has a particular resonance today when there has been a marked upsurge in interest in genealogy, with increasing numbers of people curious to trace their family roots.

Main sources for genealogical research include census returns and official records of births, marriages and deaths – and the key to unlocking the detail they contain is obviously a family surname, one that has been 'inherited' and passed from generation to generation.

No matter our station in life, we all have a surname – but it was not until about the middle of the fourteenth century that the practice of being identified by a particular surname became commonly established throughout the British Isles.

Previous to this, it was normal for a person to be identified through the use of only a forename.

But as population gradually increased and there were many more people with the same forename, surnames were adopted to distinguish one person, or community, from another.

Many common English surnames are patronymic in origin, meaning they stem from the forename of one's father – with 'Johnson,' for example, indicating 'son of John.'

It was the Normans, in the wake of their eleventh century conquest of Anglo-Saxon England, a pivotal moment in the nation's history, who first brought surnames into usage – although it was a gradual process.

For the Normans, these were names initially based on the title of their estates, local villages and chateaux in France to distinguish and identify these landholdings.

Such grand descriptions also helped enhance the prestige of these warlords and generally glorify their lofty positions high above the humble serfs slaving away below in the pecking order who had only single names, often with Biblical connotations as in Pierre and Jacques.

The only descriptive distinctions among the peasantry concerned their occupations, like 'Pierre the swineherd' or 'Jacques the ferryman.'

Roots of surnames that came into usage in England not only included Norman-French, but also Old French, Old Norse, Old English, Middle English, German, Latin, Greek, Hebrew and the Gaelic languages of the Celts.

The Normans themselves were originally Vikings, or 'Northmen', who raided, colonised and eventually settled down around the French coastline.

The had sailed up the Seine in their longboats in 900AD under their ferocious leader Rollo and ruled the roost in north eastern France before sailing over to conquer England in 1066 under Duke William of Normandy – better known to posterity as William the Conqueror, or King William I of England.

Granted lands in the newly-conquered England, some of their descendants later acquired territories in Wales, Scotland and Ireland – taking not only their own surnames, but also the practice of adopting a surname, with them.

But it was in England where Norman rule and custom first impacted, particularly in relation to the adoption of surnames.

This is reflected in the famous *Domesday Book*, a massive survey of much of England and Wales, ordered by William I, to determine who owned what, what it was worth and therefore how much they were liable to pay in taxes to the voracious Royal Exchequer.

Completed in 1086 and now held in the National Archives in Kew, London, 'Domesday' was an Old English word meaning 'Day of Judgement.'

This was because, in the words of one contemporary chronicler, "its decisions, like those of the Last Judgement, are unalterable."

It had been a requirement of all those English landholders – from the richest to the poorest – that they identify themselves for the purposes of the survey and for future reference by means of a surname.

This is why the *Domesday Book*, although written in Latin as was the practice for several centuries with both civic and ecclesiastical records, is an invaluable source for the early appearance of a wide range of English surnames.

Several of these names were coined in connection with occupations.

These include Baker and Smith, while Cooks, Chamberlains, Constables and Porters were to be found carrying out duties in large medieval households.

The church's influence can be found in names such as Bishop, Friar and Monk while the popular name of Bennett derives from the late fifth to mid-sixth century Saint Benedict, founder of the Benedictine order of monks.

The early medical profession is represented by Barber, while businessmen produced names that include Merchant and Sellers.

Down at the village watermill, the names that cropped up included Millar/Miller, Walker and Fuller, while other self-explanatory trades included Cooper, Tailor, Mason and Wright.

Even the scenery was utilised as in Moor, Hill, Wood and Forrest – while the hunt and the chase supplied names that include Hunter, Falconer, Fowler and Fox.

Colours are also a source of popular surnames, as in Black, Brown, Gray/Grey, Green and White, and would have denoted the colour of the clothing the person habitually wore or, apart from the obvious exception of 'Green', one's hair colouring or even complexion.

The surname Red developed into Reid, while

Blue was rare and no-one wanted to be associated with yellow.

Rather self-important individuals took surnames that include Goodman and Wiseman, while physical attributes crept into surnames such as Small and Little.

Many families proudly boast the heraldic device known as a Coat of Arms, as featured on our front cover.

The central motif of the Coat of Arms would originally have been what was borne on the shield of a warrior to distinguish himself from others on the battlefield.

Not featured on the Coat of Arms, but highlighted on page three, is the family motto and related crest – with the latter frequently different from the central motif.

Adding further variety to the rich cultural heritage that is represented by surnames is the appearance in recent times in lists of the 100 most common names found in England of ones that include Khan, Patel and Singh – names that have proud roots in the vast sub-continent of India.

Echoes of a far distant past can still be found in our surnames and they can be borne with pride in commemoration of our forebears.

Chapter two:

Civil war and radicals

An occupational surname derived from the Old English 'hunta', meaning 'hunter', 'Hunt' is a surname originally borne by someone who earned their living as a huntsman, or hunter.

These 'hunters' would have been employed on royal estates or on the estates and parklands of other wealthy landowners, while the important and trusted post was often hereditary.

In common with many other popular surnames found in England today, Hunt is of ancient Anglo-Saxon roots.

This means that flowing through the veins of many bearers of the name may well be the blood of those Germanic tribes who invaded and settled in the south and east of the island of Britain from about the early fifth century.

Known as the Anglo-Saxons, they were composed of the Jutes, from the area of the Jutland Peninsula in modern Denmark, the Saxons from Lower Saxony, in modern Germany and the Angles from the Angeln area of Germany.

The name is first found in Shropshire, while a Humphrey le Hunt is recorded in Sussex in 1203 and a Ralph Hunte recorded much further north, in Yorkshire, in 1219.

It is a name that features prominently in the frequently turbulent historical record.

Born in Dorset in 1609, Robert Hunt was the lawyer and politician who was a noted supporter of the Parliamentary cause during the bitter seventeenth century English Civil War.

The Catholic monarch Charles I had incurred the wrath of Parliament by his insistence on the 'divine right' of kings, and added to this was Parliament's fear of Catholic 'subversion' against the state and the king's stubborn refusal to grant demands for religious and constitutional concessions.

Matters came to a head with the outbreak of the Civil War in 1642, with Parliamentary forces, known as the New Model Army and commanded by Oliver Cromwell and Sir Thomas Fairfax, arrayed against the Royalist army of the king.

In what became an increasingly bloody and complex conflict, spreading to Scotland and Ireland and with rapidly shifting loyalties on both sides, the king was eventually captured and executed in January of 1649 on the orders of Parliament.

Qualified as a lawyer and serving as a sheriff for Somerset, Robert Hunt was placed in charge of the trial of Royalists following the abortive Penruddock Rising of March 1655.

This was when a group of Royalist conspirators, known as the Sealed Knot, planned to seize Winchester, York, Salisbury and Newcastle in the name of Charles II and also foment uprisings in Cheshire and Nottinghamshire.

But at all of these locations, apart from Salisbury, they abandoned the plan and disbanded because of the lack of necessary support. The Earl of Rochester, for example, who had travelled from the exiled court of Charles II, eventually fled back to the Continent.

But Colonel John Penruddock, along with Sir Joseph Wagstaffe, in command of 400 Royalist cavaliers, managed to take Salisbury and raise the Royal Standard.

Then marching west to gather more supporters, they were defeated by a New Model Army commanded by Captain Unton Cook after a vicious three-hour street battle in South Molton, Devon.

Those Royalists not killed or wounded managed to flee, but Penruddock and other leaders of the uprising were captured.

After a trial presided over by Robert Hunt – one that he is said to have conducted with "reliability and impartiality", Penruddock was found guilty of treason in May of 1658, and executed, while other convicted Royalists were also either executed or shipped off to the steaming plantations of the West Indies.

Hunt died in 1680, twenty years after the Restoration of Charles II.

During the late seventeenth and early eighteenth century agitation for Parliamentary reform, Henry Hunt was a noted radical speaker.

Known as "Orator" Hunt because of the rousing speeches he delivered at mass rallies throughout England, he was born in 1774 in Upavon, Wiltshire.

A prosperous farmer, he was nevertheless drawn into radical politics and, attacking what he perceived as the complacency of both the Tory and Whig political parties, called for reform that included universal suffrage and annual parliaments.

Rather than calling for violent action to achieve these goals, Hunt favoured 'mass pressure.'

To the alarm of the authorities, he had addressed mass meetings in Spa Fields, London, in 1816 and 1817 – but the largest meeting took place on August 16, 1819, at St Peter's Fields, Manchester.

Attended by up to 60,000 people, and in what became known as the Peterloo Massacre, nine men and two women were killed when a panicked militia of yeomanry who had been ordered by the authorities to arrest Hunt opened fire on the crowd.

Although blame for the killings lay entirely at the door of the authorities, the crowd having remained orderly before the militia opened fire, Hunt was arrested and sentenced to two years in prison for incitement to riot.

During his incarceration, he put pen to paper on his views on reform and how to achieve it, in addition to writing his autobiography.

In the slightly more tolerant political climate of 1830, he was elected MP for Preston, but was defeated for re-election three years later.

A year before this, in 1832, the landmark Reform Act was passed – but Hunt was not satisfied with its provisions, believing it did not go far enough to extend the franchise.

He died in 1835, while in 1842 a monument

to him was erected by "the working people" in Every Street, Manchester – but it had to be demolished nearly fifty years later because of the badly deteriorated condition of its stonework.

Recognised as responsible for a tradition that attaches to this day to the Chancellor of the Exchequer's 'Red Box', George Ward Hunt was the British Conservative party politician born in 1825 in Buckhurst, Berkshire.

Entering the House of Commons in 1857 as MP for Northamptonshire North, he served as a Secretary of the Treasury from 1866 to 1868 under Prime Minister the Earl of Derby.

It was while serving as Chancellor of the Exchequer under Prime Minister Benjamin Disraeli that, about to present his first Budget speech to the Commons, he realised that he had left his Ministerial 'Red Box' containing his speech at home.

This led to the tradition that, when the Chancellor leaves No. 11 Downing Street for the Commons on Budget Day, he displays the box to those assembled outside by holding it aloft; later appointed First Lord of the Admiralty under Disraeli, he died in 1877.

In contemporary British politics, David Hunt,

born in 1942 in Glyn Ceiriog, Wales and elevated to
the Peerage of the United Kingdom as Baron Hunt of
Wirral, is the Conservative Party politician who was
appointed Secretary of State for Wales in 1990 under
the Premiership of Margaret Thatcher.

Remaining in this post until 1993, he later
served for a time as Secretary of State for Employment.

Chapter three:

Tycoons and adventurers

An impressive number of bearers of the Hunt name have stamped their mark on the historical record as highly successful entrepreneurs.

Born in 1817 in Brownsville, Fayette County, Pennsylvania, Alfred Hunt served as the first president of the Bethlehem Iron Company – forerunner of today's Bethlehem Steel Corporation.

Beginning his career in the iron and steel industry in 1849 through the firm of Rowland and Hunt, based in Cheltenham Township, Pennsylvania, he later formed a business partnership with John C. Fremont that led to the creation of the Bethlehem Iron Company.

He remained president of the company until his death in 1888.

The founder in the late nineteenth century of what remains today the world's biggest producer and distributor of aluminium, Alfred Ephraim Hunt, better known as Alfred E. Hunt, was the American metallurgist and industrialist born in New England in 1855.

Graduating from the Massachusetts Institute of Technology (MIT) in 1876 with a degree in metallurgy and mining, he worked for a number of iron and steel companies across the United States before in 1887, along with George Hubbard Clapp, taking over the Pittsburgh Testing Laboratory.

The partners then made the acquaintance of the young chemist Charles Hall, who had been awarded a patent for a process for separating aluminium from aluminium oxide through electrolysis.

The process, named the Hall-Héroult process because of the contribution also made to it by the chemist Paul Héroult, was put into effect on an industrial scale by Hall, Clapp and a number of other business partners.

Launching the Pittsburgh Reduction Company to produce the aluminium, Hall later renamed it Aluminium Company of America – later shortened to Alcoa, the name by which it is known today; he died in 1899.

One particularly colourful bearer of the Hunt name was Haroldson Lafayette Hunt, Jr., the Texas oil tycoon better known as H.L. Hunt.

Born in 1899 in Carson Township, Fayette County, Illinois, the son of a prosperous farmer and entrepreneur, by the time he was aged 23 he was running his own cotton plantation in Arkansas.

Known for his mathematical brain, he was also an inveterate gambler and when his plantation was ruined by floods he turned his last $100 into more than $10,000 dollars by gambling in New Orleans.

He used his winnings to buy oil properties in the El Dorado area of Arkansas, while he later secured the rights to what became known as the East Texas Oil Field.

Containing massive reserves of oil, this field made Hunt so wealthy that on his death in 1974 he was reputed to have had amassed the highest net worth of any individual in the world.

In 1957, seventeen years before his death, *Fortune* magazine had estimated his fortune to be between $400million and $700million – worth approximately $4.5billion in today's terms.

The Texas city of Hunt is named after him, while his colourful personal life – including having fathered fifteen children to three wives – was one of the main inspirations for the character of the oil tycoon J.R. Ewing in the popular television series *Dallas*.

He was the father of Nelson Bunker Hunt,

born in 1926, the oil company executive and thoroughbred racehorse breeder who lost his fortune after he and his brother William Herbert Hunt, born in 1929, attempted to corner the world market in silver.

Chairman of Hunt Exploration and Mining Company, he and his brother began accumulating vast amounts of silver in the early 1970s, to the extent that by 1979 they had nearly cornered the global market.

They profited by an estimated $4billion in silver speculation, with prices of silver bullion rising from $11 an ounce to $50 an ounce by the beginning of 1980.

But the profitable bubble burst when silver prices eventually collapsed to below $11 an ounce in March of 1980 – with the largest single day drop in the price occurring in what became known as Silver Thursday.

Hunt was declared bankrupt, fined $10million and banned from trading in the commodity markets for conspiring to manipulate the silver market.

Earlier, as a leading racehorse breeder, he was the British flat racing champion in both 1973 and 1974 and winner of the 1976 Epsom Derby.

His brother, Lamar Hunt, born in 1932, was a major promoter in America of soccer, as European football is known there, American football, basketball, tennis and ice hockey.

A founder of the American Football League (AFL) and Major League Soccer (MSL) and co-founder of World Championship tennis, he died in 2006.

His son, Clark Knobel Hunt, born in 1965, has followed in his father's sporting footsteps. Chairman and chief executive of the American football team the Kansas City Chiefs, he is also chairman of the Hunt Sports Group.

One adventurous bearer of the name was Henry Hunt, leader of the successful 1953 expedition to scale Mount Everest.

Born in 1910 in Simla, India, the son of a British captain in the Indian army and a great nephew of the famous explorer Sir Francis Burton, he was aged only 14 when he made a guided ascent of Piz Palu in the Himalayas.

Appointed a military intelligence officer with the Indian Army in 1934, he indulged his passion for mountain climbing in his spare time.

In 1935, as a member of a group led by the British climber James Waller, he reached 24,500ft. while attempting to scale the formidable Saltoro

Kangri in the Himalayas – a feat which earned him election to the prestigious Alpine Club and the Royal Geographical Society.

Serving during the Second World War as chief instructor at the Commando Mountain and Snow Warfare School in Braemar, Scotland, he later served on the staff of Supreme Headquarters Allied Expeditionary Force (SHAEF).

Selected as leader of the British assault on Mount Everest in 1953, it was in April of that year that he established base camp.

He had selected two climbing parties to attempt the final assault on the summit, and it was the one led by the New Zealander Edmund Hillary, along with the Nepalese Sherpa Tenzing Norgay that reached it on May 29; both Hunt and Hillary were knighted for their efforts.

Hunt also accrued, before his death in 1998, other honours that included the granting of the title of Baron Hunt, while he also later served as the first director of the Duke of Edinburgh Award Scheme.

In addition to this, his advisory role for the government in the policing of Northern Ireland culminated in the *Hunt Report*, recommending the disbandment of the quasi-military police force the B-

Specials and its replacement with the Ulster Defence Regiment.

Born in 1926 in Redcar, in the North Riding of Yorkshire, Sir Rex Hunt was the governor of the British sovereign territory of the Falkland Islands when it was invaded and occupied by Argentinian forces in 1982.

With no option but give the order to the small detachment of Royal Marines to lay down their arms, Sir Rex was expelled by the Argentinians – but he returned as governor following the recapture of the islands and remained in the post until 1985.

Author of the 1992 *My Falkland Days* and portrayed by the actor Ian Richardson in the 1992 BBC Television drama *An Ungentlemanly Act*, he died in 2012.

Chapter four:

On the world stage

Born in Covent Garden, London, in 1954, David Hunt is the British actor whose first major film role was as the murderer Harlan Rook in the 1988 *The Dead Pool* – the fifth instalment in the Dirty Harry series.

Other film credits include the 1991 *The Black Velvet Gown*, the 2001 *Murder on the Orient Express* and, from 2008, *The Deal*.

Married to the American actress Patricia Heaton, star of the television sitcom *Everybody Loves Raymond*, in which he has had guest roles, other television credits include *24*, *Monk* and *Mad Men*.

Not only an actress but also a comedian, writer, director, television producer and talk show host, **Bonnie Hunt** was born in Chicago in 1961.

An oncology nurse before taking to the stage as a career, she was a founder in 1984 of an improvisational comedy troupe while she also performed with Chicago's *Second City* comedy group.

On the big screen, her major credits include the 1988 *Rain Man*, the 1995 *Jumani* – for which she won a Saturn Award for Best Supporting Actress – and the 2000 *Return to Me*, which she also co-wrote and directed. From 2008 to 2010 she was also host of the daytime talk show *The Bonnie Hunt Show*, for which she won a Daytime Emmy Award for Outstanding Talk Show Host.

Blacklisted from Hollywood studios in the early 1950s, along with others connected to the film industry because of their alleged left wing sympathies, Marcia Virginia Hunt is the American actress better known as **Marsha Hunt**.

Born in Chicago in 1917, she had worked as a singer and model before being signed to Paramount Pictures when aged 17.

Her film debut came a year later in the 1935 *The Virginia Judge*, while other film credits throughout the 1930s and 1940s include the 1936 *Hollywood Boulevard* and the 1948 *The Raw Deal*.

Having signed a number of petitions that promoted liberal causes in the United States, she found herself blacklisted from Hollywood during the anti-Communist hysteria of the early 1950s.

Once the 'Reds under the Bed' scare had run its course, her career revived – starring in films that include the 1955 *A Word to the Wives* and the 1959

Blue Denim; she also has a number of television credits that include *Star Trek: The Next Generation*.

Only 4ft. 9in. in height, Lydia Susanna Hunter is the American actress better known as **Linda Hunt**.

Born in 1945 in Morristown, New Jersey, she is best known for her role of Billy Kwan in the 1982 film *The Year of Living Dangerously* – for which she won an Academy Award for Best Supporting Actress – and as Henrietta Lange in the television series *NCIS: Los Angeles*.

Other film credits include the 1980 *Popeye*, the 1984 *The Bostonians* and, from 2006, *Stranger than Fiction*.

A merchant seaman before taking to the stage, Alan Leonard Hunt was the English actor better known as **Gareth Hunt**.

Born in 1942 in Battersea, London, he joined the Royal Shakespeare Company after leaving the Merchant Navy – his reason for leaving being that he had jumped ship while in New Zealand and subsequently spent time in prison for this.

His television career began in the early 1970s with roles in Doctor Who and the sitcom *Bless this House* – but he is best known for his role in 1972 as the footman Frederick Norton in the period drama

Upstairs Downstairs and as Mike Gambit in the 1976 series *The New Avengers*.

With roles in other British television series that include *Hammer House of Mystery and Suspense*, *Minder*, *New Tricks* and *Doctors*, he died in 2007.

Behind the camera lens, Peter Roger Hunt, better known as **Peter R. Hunt**, was the film director and editor best known for his work on six of the *James Bond* films. As an editor, he was involved with the 1962 *Dr No*, the 1963 *From Russia with Love*, the 1964 *Goldfinger*, the 1965 *Thunderball* and 1967's *You Only Live Twice* – while he directed the 1969 *On Her Majesty's Secret Service*.

Born in London in 1925 and also having been involved in a number of other films that include the 1976 *Shout at the Devil*, he died in 2002.

Not only a presenter of history programmes on television but also a British Labour Party politician, **Tristram Hunt**, born in 1974 and who was elected MP for Stoke-on-Trent Central in 2012, has presented programmes that include the 2002 *The English Civil War*. He is also the author of a number of books that include his 2009 *The Frock-Coated Communist: The Revolutionary Life of Friedrich Engels*.

Bearers of the Hunt name have also excelled

in the highly competitive world of sport – no less so than the late British Formula One motor racing champion **James Hunt**.

Born in 1947 in Sutton, Surrey, the son of a stock broker, his racing career began in touring car racing.

Progressing to Formula 3, he was taken up by the Hesketh Racing Team and entered Formula One in 1973, moving two years later to the McLaren Team.

It was with McLaren that he won the World Drivers' Championship in the year he joined them, while his crowning glory came in 1976 when he won the Formula One World Championship.

Nicknamed "Hunt the Shunt" because of his on-track exploits, he left McLaren for the Wolf Team in 1979, but retired halfway through the season and went on to become a popular BBC commentator on the sport in addition to pursuing a number of business interests. Noted for his rebellious spirit and unconventional lifestyle, he was known for dining in expensive London Mayfair restaurants with his pet Alsatian dog.

In 1977, at a special gala function attended by the Duke of Kent, the carefree Hunt raised more than a few eyebrows when he arrived to receive the Tarmac Trophy dressed in denims, a t-shirt and a scruffy windcheater.

He died from a heart attack in 1993, while he was the older brother of former racing driver **David Hunt**, born in 1960. Competing in the Formula Three Championship from 1983 to 1987, he bought what was then the bankrupt Lotus Team in 1994, but sold the rights to the Lotus name in 2009 to the Litespeed Formula Three Team.

From the motor racing track to the sea, **David Hunt**, born in 1934, is the British sailor who, with Alan Warren, won the silver medal in the Tempest Class at the 1972 Olympics.

In badminton, **Chris Hunt**, born in 1968, is the British retired badminton player who, along with Simon Archer, won the gold medal in the men's doubles at the 1994 and 1998 Olympics.

From sport to music, **Marsha Hunt** is the American singer, actress, model and writer best known as a cast member of the original London stage production of the rock musical *Hair*.

Born in Philadelphia in 1946, she worked as a singer for nearly two years before moving to Britain in 1966 and singing for a time with Alexis Korner's trio Free at Last and later with the band Ferris Wheel. But she rose to fame in 1968 through her role of Dione in *Hair* – with her photograph being used on the iconic poster and playbill of the original London production.

She graced the cover of the British fashion magazine *Queen* three months after *Hair* opened, making her the first black model to do so.

She also posed, naked, for the photographer Patrick Lichfield in 1968 for the cover of *Vogue* magazine, and was photographed in the same pose forty years later – after she had undergone surgery for breast cancer; this photograph appears on the cover of her autobiography *Undefeated*.

Hit singles she recorded include the 1969 *Walk on Gilded Splinters*, while she has also collaborated with musicians who include Marc Bolan, Long John Baldry, John Mayall and Elton John. Once romantically linked to Mick Jagger, she is also the author of novels that include her 1990 *Joy* and the 1992 *Free*, while film credits include the 1982 *Britannia Hospital*.

Not only a top level diplomat but also a noted British television quiz contestant, **Sir David Hunt** was born in 1913 in Durham. Having studied at Wadham College, Oxford and serving with distinction during the Second World War, he entered the diplomatic service in 1947 and later served as Private Secretary to Prime Ministers Clement Attlee and Winston Churchill.

Knighted in 1963, he served as British High

Commissioner to Cyprus from 1965 to 1967 and then as British Ambassador to Brazil.

He won BBC Television's *Mastermind* title in 1977, four years after he retired, while in 1979 he was runner-up in *Mastermind International*, and in 1982 winner of the Champion of Champions title – that had involved a contest among the first ten *Mastermind* winners. Author of a number of books that include his 1990 *Footprints in Cyprus*, he died in 1998.

In the highly creative world of art, **William Holman Hunt**, born in 1827 in Cheapside, London was the English painter who along with Dante Gabriel Rossetti and John Everett Millais was a founder in 1848 of the Pre-Raphaelite movement.

Famous for paintings that include his *The Light of the World*, *The Scapegoat* and *The Shadow of Death*, he died in 1910, while he was portrayed by the actor Rafe Spall in the BBC television drama on the Pre-Raphaelites, *Desperate Romantics*.

One daredevil bearer of the Hunt name was William Leonard Hunt, better known as the acrobat and stuntman **The Great Farini**. Born in 1838 in Lockport, New York but moving as a teenager with his family to Hope Township, Ontario, his most famous feats took place in August of 1860.

This was when he crossed the Niagara Falls on a high wire with a man on his back.

As if this was not daring enough, he also crossed the falls with a sack over his head, while another stunt involved turning somersaults on the wire.

The Great Farini, in addition to becoming in 1885 the first person recorded as having crossed the Kalahari Desert on foot, also invented the apparatus used in the 'human cannonball" feat; he died in 1929.

One particularly inventive bearer of the proud name of Hunt was the American mechanic **Walter Hunt**, born in 1796 in Martinsburg, New York.

In addition to inventing the fountain pen, a forerunner of the Winchester repeating rifle, a knife sharpener, street sweeping machine and the ice plough, he also invented, in 1833, the lockstitch sewing machine and, in 1849, the safety pin.

Unaware of the significance of many of his inventions, he sold the patent for the safety pin for only $400, worth about $10,000 at today's value, to W.R. Grace and Company.

He did not even bother to patent his lockstitch sewing machine – troubled that it would create unemployment for seamstresses.

The mechanical genius died in 1859.